Contents

MEET KING ALFRED THE GREAT

Alfred was the only English king ever to be given the title 'Great', even though he was never in fact king of the whole of England. To find out how Alfred earned his title, we need to look at the story of his life.

Who was Alfred?

Alfred was the youngest son of Aethelwulf, the king of Wessex (see page 5), and his first wife, Osburh. His mother died while Alfred was still a child. Alfred had four older brothers, so he was not expected to become king. Sadly, all his brothers died while they were still young.

When did Alfred live?

Alfred was born in CE 849. At this time, England was settled by the Anglo-Saxons. The Anglo-Saxons were farmers and fierce warriors. They came to England from northern Europe after the Romans left Britain in around 410.

This statue of King Alfred stands in the city of Winchester.

Where did Alfred live?

Alfred was born in England. At that time England was divided into five main regions – Northumbria, East Anglia, Kent, Mercia and Wessex. Each region had a different king. Alfred became king of Wessex when he was just 22 years old. Wessex covered most of the south of England. Its capital was the town of Winchester and this is where Alfred spent most of his time.

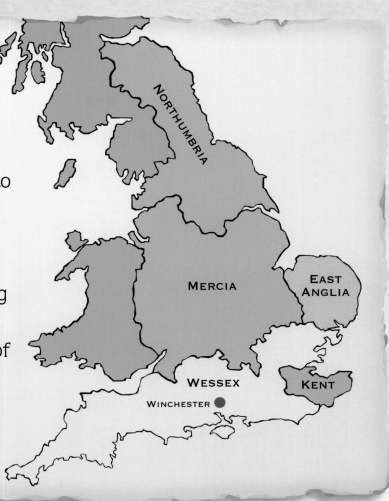

NORTHUMBRIA

MERCIA

EAST ANGLIA

WESSEX

KENT

WINCHESTER

Why was Alfred given the title 'Great'?

Alfred is most famous for saving England from being conquered. Throughout his life, Alfred battled with the Vikings, who attacked England to gain land and riches. To help defeat the Vikings, Alfred formed the first English army and navy. Alfred also encouraged his people to speak and write in their own language rather than Latin. English is now one of the most commonly-used languages in the world, thanks partly to Alfred.

The Vikings sailed to Britain from the countries of Scandinavia – Norway, Denmark and Sweden.

ALFRED'S LIFE STORY

By the time Alfred was 22 years old, he had travelled across Europe, he had seen his parents and his four brothers die, he had faced death fighting the Vikings and now he was to be crowned king of Wessex. Alfred would have many more adventures in the following years.

1 ALFRED VISITS ROME TO MEET THE POPE WHEN HE IS JUST FOUR YEARS OLD.

ONE DAY YOU WILL BE A KING.

2

ALFRED MY SON, THIS IS YOURS TO KEEP.

ALFRED RECEIVES A SPECIAL POETRY BOOK AS A PRIZE FROM HIS MOTHER. HE LOVES TO READ AND TO LEARN.

3 ALFRED'S MUM DIES WHEN HE IS JUST EIGHT YEARS OLD.

4

GIVE ME GOLD AND SILVER AND I WILL NOT HARM YOUR PEOPLE.

ALFRED WATCHES IVAR THE BONELESS, LEADER OF THE GREAT VIKING ARMY, SIGN A PEACE AGREEMENT WITH BURGHRED, KING OF MERCIA.

5

Young Alfred leads his brother's army to a famous victory over the Vikings at the Battle of Ashdown.

6

Alfred becomes king of Wessex at the age of 22 when his brother Athelred dies.

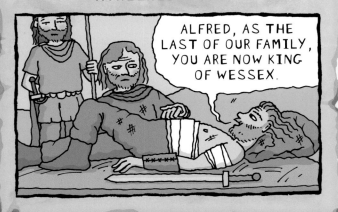

7

Alfred defeats the great Viking leader Guthrum at the Battle of Edington.

8

Alfred protects important English towns from Viking attack.

9

To make the country safer, Alfred forms the first permanent English army and navy.

10

In later life, Alfred arranges for many books to be translated into English and translates some himself.

ALFRED VISITS ROME

Alfred and his family were Christians and the leader of the Christian Church is the Pope, who lives in Rome. When Alfred was four years old, his father Aethelwulf sent him on a pilgrimage to Rome to meet Pope Leo IV.

Young Alfred kneels in front of Pope Leo IV.

The road to Rome

Alfred's journey to Rome was long, slow and dangerous, but he had bodyguards to protect him. The meeting with the Pope was a great success. The Pope was so impressed with Alfred that he became Alfred's godfather. It is also claimed that the Pope told Alfred that he would be a king one day.

HISTORY LINKS

St Peter's Basilica (church) is one of the most famous buildings in Rome. It is named after Peter, a follower of Jesus who is thought to have been crucified where St Peter's Basilica is built. Alfred would have seen the very first church of St Peter. It was replaced in 1506 by the church we can see in Rome today (below).

A second trip to Rome

King Aethelwulf

Alfred's mother, Osburh, died soon after Alfred's return from Rome. This may have prompted Aethelwulf to go on his own pilgrimage. He took Alfred with him, but when they arrived in Rome they were met with the sad news that Pope Leo IV had died.

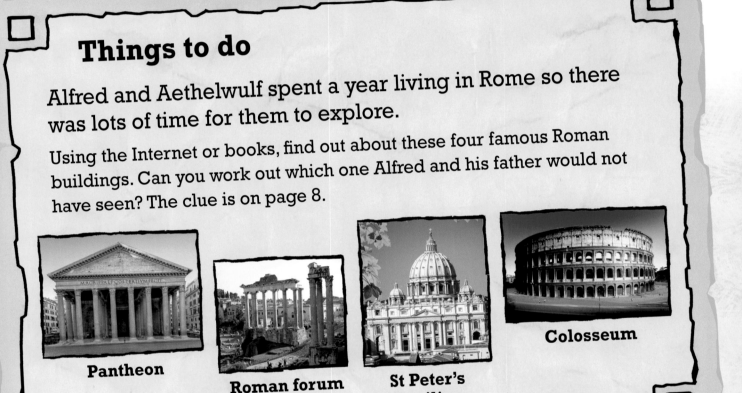

Things to do

Alfred and Aethelwulf spent a year living in Rome so there was lots of time for them to explore.

Using the Internet or books, find out about these four famous Roman buildings. Can you work out which one Alfred and his father would not have seen? The clue is on page 8.

Pantheon

Roman forum

St Peter's Basilica

Colosseum

Aethelwulf gets married again

On the way home from Rome, Aethelwulf stopped off to get married to Judith of France, the great granddaughter of the famous Emperor Charlemagne. Their marriage strengthened the bonds between France and England, which were both suffering from Viking attacks.

9

FIGHTING THE VIKINGS

Vikings raiders were feared all along the coast of Britain.

Vikings had been raiding places along the east coast of Britain since the end of the 8th century. They targeted churches and monasteries where there were valuable items to steal and only monks to stop them. Alfred would have heard all about the very first Viking raid on the Holy Island of Lindisfarne in 793.

THE SAXON CHRONICLE

9 June 793

Yesterday, 8 June 793, is a day for all of us to remember and to fear. Monks on the Holy Island of Lindisfarne were going about their daily tasks, when, from out of nowhere, strange ships landed on the sandy beach nearby. Viking men from across the seas had brought evil to this quiet, godly place.

Monks were cruelly hacked down by sword and axe, some were drowned and others were taken away to be sold as slaves.

These Vikings care nothing for the things of God. They stole every precious thing they could lay their hands on. It is terrible to think that those beautiful items which had been dedicated to God are now in the hands of pagan thugs.

Take care all you God-fearing Christians because we have not heard the last of these Viking raiders!

The Battle of Edington

In 865 a Viking army invaded England. It marched across the country, defeating the Anglo-Saxons again and again. In the end, only Alfred and his men were left to carry on fighting the Vikings. With an army of 4,000 men Alfred faced the Viking leader Guthrum and his army at a place called Edington. Against all the odds, they won a great victory. Instead of killing Guthrum, Alfred made him agree to be baptised into the Christian Church, showing he could be both wise and merciful.

Alfred (seated) baptises Guthrum as a Christian.

YORK

DANELAW

LONDON

EDINGTON

SOUTH OF ENGLAND

The Danelaw was so-called because the Danes (another name for the Vikings) ruled and made the laws there.

Danelaw

In the days following the Battle of Edington, Alfred and Guthrum agreed a peace treaty which divided England roughly in half. Alfred ruled the south of England and the Vikings ruled East Anglia and Northumbria. The land where the Vikings ruled was called the Danelaw.

11

ALFRED AND THE CAKES

This legend from Alfred's life tells the story behind Alfred's famous victory at the Battle of Edington.

Alfred is 28 years old and he has been king for seven years. It is Monday, 6 January, Twelfth Night, the end of the Christmas feast. Alfred has been celebrating Christmas in a town called Chippenham with his family, friends and closest advisors. Alfred has no idea that a Viking army is on its way to capture him and take control of England.

'Thank you my Lord.' Thane (Lord) Edwin got to his feet and bowed before his king. He took the heavy, silver ring he had just been given and pushed it proudly onto his arm.

As Edwin returned to his family, Alfred looked around the great hall at the many people gathered there. He knew all of them by name. Alfred raised his hand and the crowd grew silent. He apologised to them all, but he was not feeling well. Not for the first time, he was troubled by pains in his gut.

Troubled sleep

Alfred did not sleep well that night. Something was wrong. He noticed it in the way some of his men had looked at him during the feast – as if they were keeping something from him. As Alfred was drifting off, the door opened and two men slipped into his room.

'My Lord, you must get dressed, the enemy has been seen close by. We should leave immediately.'

'No! We will stay and fight. Sound the alarm, order the men to the gates.'

Thane Edwin hesitated. 'We cannot rely on their loyalty. Quickly, my Lord, Guthrum and his Viking army are almost upon us.'

Alfred said nothing more. He knew now the danger he was in and escape was all that mattered. Within minutes Alfred and a few trusted men were riding like the wind across the heath and out over the high moors.

By the time morning came Alfred was safe, but his heart was broken. It was clear that some of his own people had betrayed him.

Hiding in the marshes

Later that day Alfred reached Athelney. It was a place of reeds and marsh and deep, deep mud that would suck the life from any lost traveller. But it was a place Alfred knew well from his childhood. The treacherous marshes would be his defence.

Alfred and his men reached the house on the edge of the marsh when the Sun was high overhead. It was a place they had rested at before. The family were Anglo-Saxon, just like Alfred. He trusted them with his life.

As his men sharpened their weapons outside, Alfred sat staring at the oatcakes as they cooked in the heat of the fire. He thought back to the time when people looked to him as their leader. Now he felt like little more than an outlaw. Doubt crept into his thoughts. He felt weak and powerless.

'Look what you have done!' shouted the woman. 'The cakes are burnt. Do you think we have enough food to waste?'

Alfred looked up and saw the anger on the woman's face. 'Forgive me, my mind was on other things,' he replied.

'Fat lot of good that will do us. We need men of action, men of daring, not men lost in idle thinking.' Alfred was jolted to his feet. She was right and he knew it.

Alfred smiled. 'Come,' he said. 'Let us eat together and then we must be on our way, for we have a war to win.'

Within a few short weeks Alfred had gathered an army of about 4,000 men who would go on to win the most important battle of their lives. Is the story of Alfred burning the cakes true? We cannot be sure. Some of the details of the story may not be accurate but we do know Alfred was nearly captured at Chippenham and he certainly won a great and unexpected victory at the Battle of Edington.

THE GROWTH OF TOWNS

At the time of King Alfred, most people in England lived in villages or small market towns. When the Vikings moved inland they found most towns were easy to seize. Alfred decided to do something to protect his people.

Under Alfred, many important towns became much better defended.

Fortress towns

Alfred chose over thirty of the biggest, most important towns across the south of England and made each one into a fortress. A wall or a wooden fence was built around the outside of the town and ditches were dug around them to make the town harder to attack. Alfred's plan was for everyone to be able to reach a fortress town within a day's walk. He also made sure there would always be trained soldiers there ready and waiting to fight off a Viking attack.

Burhs

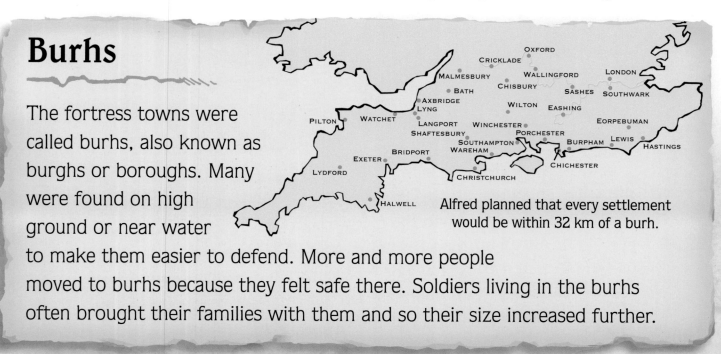

The fortress towns were called burhs, also known as burghs or boroughs. Many were found on high ground or near water to make them easier to defend. More and more people moved to burhs because they felt safe there. Soldiers living in the burhs often brought their families with them and so their size increased further.

Alfred planned that every settlement would be within 32 km of a burh.

London

When Alfred was king, Winchester was his capital but London was still very important. It is easy to see why. London is close to the sea and the River Thames, which runs through London, stretches out into the heart of England. The Vikings tried many times to take control of London, but in 886 Alfred finally drove them out of the city. He rebuilt London's Roman walls and created a new centre. New streets were created on a grid pattern. He also had jetties built along the river so it was easy for goods to be loaded on and off boats.

From Roman times up to the present day, London has been a very important settlement.

HISTORY LINKS

ABOUT 800 YEARS BEFORE THE TIME OF ALFRED, WHEN THE SOUTH OF ENGLAND WAS UNDER ROMAN RULE, LONDON WAS ATTACKED BY QUEEN BOUDICA, LEADER OF THE ICENI TRIBE. HER ARMY BURNED LONDON TO THE GROUND AND MURDERED ANY ROMAN CITIZEN THEY COULD FIND THERE.

Things to do

Many towns and cities are built next to a river. This is also true of the burhs that Alfred built. Below is a list of ten capital cities from around the world. Each one is next to a river.

Find out which river flows through these cities.

1. Paris 2. Vienna 3. Buenos Aires 4. Rome 5. Budapest
6. Khartoum 7. Baghdad 8. Ottawa 9. Cairo 10. Beijing

ALFRED THE GREAT LEARNER

Alfred achieved many great things in his life, but he always thought that the most important thing a person could do was learn. He once said, 'I cannot find anything better in man than that he know.'

Alfred the reader

As a boy, Alfred treasured the poetry book he was given as a prize by his mother. However, he did not learn how to read properly until he was an adult. From then on, Alfred liked nothing better than to sit and study books. He was interested in many things: nature, science, how things work, distant lands and most of all, what great thinkers said about worshipping God.

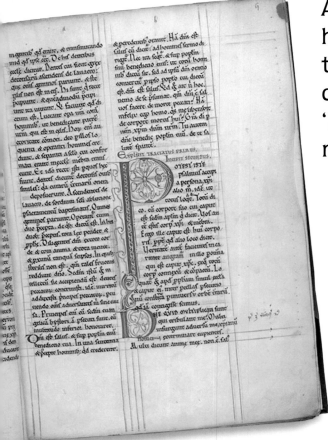

An extract from a book written by St. Augustine of Hippo, a favourite writer of Alfred the Great

Things to do

Anglo-Saxon monks illustrated their writings with patterns and pictures, especially the initial letter of a piece of writing. Young Alfred loved to look at such pictures.

Look on these pages and the Internet for examples of Anglo-Saxon writing. Try to create a similar pattern for the initial letters of your own name. Have a go at drawing a picture inside one of the letters.

Learning for leaders

Alfred wanted all the leaders in his kingdom to be able to read. If they were to carry out his instructions, leaders such as judges, generals, nobles, priests and teachers would have to be able to read them first. Alfred started a school at his own court where young leaders of the future were shown how to read, write and even how to think. They listened to Greek legends, read about great people of the past and learned the teachings of the Church.

During Alfred's lifetime, the Bible could only be read in Latin.

From Latin to English

During Alfred's reign, most books were written in Latin, the language used by the Roman Catholic Church. Alfred searched everywhere for educated men (usually monks) who could translate books from Latin to English. Alfred wanted the English people to be proud of who they were and the language they used.

Alfred sent bishops and priests instruction books along with 'pointers', (the handle of one is shown here, with Alfred's face on it) to help the priest follow the text.

17

BEOWULF

Alfred would have heard this famous Anglo-Saxon legend, originally written as a poem, from storytellers who visited his father's court. They held the audience spellbound as they made the story of Beowulf come alive.

Hrothgar, the king of Denmark, was where he loved to be, in his feasting hall making merry with all his friends. The sound of laughter from the hall drifted over the fields and out across the swamp. Something in the darkness stirred.

Slowly Grendel rose, his yellow eyes gleamed in the ghostly mist. Mud slid from his scaly body as he stood, hunched, taller than a man, wider than a tree. Once he was on the move he glided across the swamp, sometimes on all fours and then suddenly rising to his full height, long legs eating up the ground in giant steps.

By the time Grendel reached the great hall, everything lay silent. Without warning Grendel struck. Talons tore through flesh, bones snapped like dry twigs, bodies lay twisted and tangled, cast aside as if they were children's toys.

Night after night guards patrolled the great hall, sword in one hand, spear in the other. But each time Grendel came without warning, out of the shadows of the swamp, some said out of the very ground they walked on. And each time death followed in his path. A dark cloud hung over the people of Denmark.

Beowulf arrives

One day a man called Beowulf landed on the shores of Denmark. He had the heart of a lion, the strength of a bear and the cunning of a snake. The doors of the great hall were flung open to welcome this brave stranger. After the feasting Beowulf stood with his men and waited. One by one they gave in to sleep, until only Beowulf was left standing.

A howling screech pierced the silence of the night. Beowulf remained perfectly still while everything around him turned to chaos. Confused men clambered over each other in search of their weapons. The doors suddenly burst open. The beast glared at Beowulf. Two men rushed forward, wielding swords, screaming as loudly as their courage would allow. Grendel lifted them off the ground as if they were children. Beowulf jumped on a table, then on to a wooden pillar and launched himself onto Grendel's back. His strong arms wrapped themselves tight around the monster's neck. Grendel lashed out, overturning tables and chairs, twisting, turning, desperately trying to be free of the man who was clamped to his back. Beowulf grabbed hold of a beam of wood above his head and drew his legs up and around the monster's throat. All at once he twisted Grendel's body and jammed his head and shoulders between two upright wooden pillars. Grendel was stuck!

Beowulf knew he had to make the most of this moment. He jumped to the floor and grabbed hold of Grendel's arm. He pulled it backwards, behind Grendel's body. He pulled as hard as ever he could. Grendel shrieked with pain. Then, with one final pull, Beowulf tore Grendel's arm clear from his body. Beowulf held the prize high above his head, taunting Grendel, whose lifeless body crashed to the ground.

'Nail Grendel's arm to the door,' shouted Beowulf, 'so that all Danes may see that the creature's terror is at an end and the Danes can once again dance to the music of freedom.'

Alfred's Law

As soon as Alfred had made a peace agreement with the Vikings (see page 11), he began to organise his kingdom.

God's Law

Alfred introduced a new set of laws and punishments. These were based on the ten laws, or commandments, that God gave to the prophet Moses in the Bible. The Ten Commandments told people what they should do and shouldn't do, such as only worshipping one god and not stealing or telling lies. Alfred added other laws too, such as swearing an oath to the king. This meant staying loyal to the king and obeying his laws.

Alfred set out to rule his kingdom strictly, but fairly.

In some cases, innocence was tested in a 'Trial by Ordeal'. For instance, the accused had their arm scalded in hot water. If after three days the arm was healing, it was seen as a sign from God that you were innocent!

Innocent or guilty?

Alfred was the highest judge in the land and people brought him the most important disputes to settle. For local arguments and law-breaking, the people of the village often acted as judge. Witnesses gave evidence at a trial. Where it was one person's word against another, a case could be decided by how many people you could get to speak up for you.

Punishments

There were no police or prisons in the time of Alfred. Paying a fine was the most common way of punishing law-breakers. Fines could be paid 'in kind' which meant giving up something of equal value to the fine, such as a cow, some sheep or a piece of land.

Things to do

You are the judge

Below are two crimes from Anglo-Saxon times. As the judge, you must decide what happens next. Share your thinking and ideas with a friend or adult.

Godwin has worked hard to grow some barley, cabbage and other vegetables on his small patch of land. One morning he finds his crops ruined by three cows owned by Cedric, one of the wealthier villagers. Godwin complains to Cedric, but he says that there should have been a fence round the crops and he will not do anything.

How would you settle this dispute?

Ethelred and Sam have agreed to do some sword fighting practice. During the practice Ethelred is cut across the hand. He will not be able to plough his fields in time for planting. He blames Sam for being too rough, but Sam says it was just an accident.

How would you settle this dispute?

21

CHRISTIANS AND PAGANS

Like many Anglo-Saxons living in England, Alfred was a devout Christian.

Beliefs

Christians believe that there is one God and that his son, Jesus Christ, had been sent to Earth to save people from sin. The Vikings did not believe in Jesus. They were pagans who believed in many Norse gods, such as Odin, Thor and Freya.

The Viking god of thunder, Thor

An Anglo-Saxon Christmas

We can see differences between Christians and pagans in the way they celebrated one of their most important festivals. Each year on 25 December, Christians celebrate the birth of Jesus Christ. The first thing Alfred would do on Christmas Day was celebrate Mass. A priest would have given Alfred bread to represent the body of Jesus, and wine, to represent the blood of Jesus. Taking Mass was very important to Alfred. Today, Christians all over the world celebrate Christmas by giving gifts to remind them that God gave mankind the gift of his son, Jesus Christ.

The priest blesses the wine at a 9th century Mass.

A midwinter festival

In December every year, the Vikings held a midwinter festival where they celebrated the end of the darkest time of the year. They danced around a bright fire which represented the Sun, wearing masks and beating their shields to the rhythm of the dance. Storytellers would entertain people with stories about heroes and Viking gods.

Vikings called their midwinter Festival 'Yol', from which we get the word 'Yule'. Yol means wheel and was used to describe how the seasons keep going round and round.

Becoming Christian

Over the years, many Vikings who settled in Britain, as well as those at home in Scandinavia, began worshipping Jesus alongside their other gods. Eventually, most Vikings became Christians, just like the Anglo-Saxons.

Things to do

Have a go at making a Viking fire mask out of card, like the one shown here.

ALFRED'S END AND LEGACY

Alfred died on 26 October 899 when he was just 50 years old, possibly because of a longstanding stomach condition. He was buried in his capital city of Winchester.

An engraving of King Alfred the Great.

England's saviour

England owes a great debt to Alfred to this day, and he is one of its most celebrated kings. At one time in Alfred's reign, he clung on to power by his fingertips. Yet his skill, leadership and determination united his people and gave them the belief that they could defeat the Vikings. Without Alfred, the Vikings might well have conquered the whole country in the 10th century.

FASCINATING FACTS

THE NAME WESSEX MEANS 'KINGDOM OF THE WEST SAXONS.'
SAXON PEOPLE CAME FROM SAXONY, NOW PART OF GERMANY.
SAXONS GAVE THEIR NAME TO THESE ENGLISH COUNTIES:

ESSEX (KINGDOM OF THE EAST SAXONS)
SUSSEX (KINGDOM OF THE SOUTH SAXONS)
MIDDLESEX (KINGDOM OF THE MIDDLE SAXONS)

Saviour of the English language

An old drawing of Alfred studying a book.

If the Vikings had indeed conquered England, the English language might not exist. Alfred helped to keep it alive. Alfred realised that for people to 'feel' English they would need things to unite them, such as a strong king as leader and one common language. We would not be able to understand the language spoken by Alfred, but we would have recognised some Anglo-Saxon words. These words were the beginnings of the English language we use today.

Things to do

Below are some 'Old English' words that would have been used by Anglo-Saxons. Can you work out what they mean?

1. I live in this hus with my brodor.

2. She is my wif and I lufu her with all my heart.

3. I oft go ham to see my modor.

Answers on page 32

Saviour of the Christian Church

If the Vikings had defeated Alfred at the Battle of Edington in 878, England would have become a pagan country. But Alfred won and the message of the Christian faith spread to all corners of Britain, as well as parts of Europe.

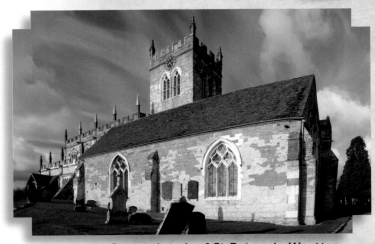

The Anglo-Saxon church of St Peters in Wootton Wawen, Warwickshire, dates back to the 8th century. The original wooden building was burned down by the Vikings, but it was rebuilt and still stands today.

ALFRED'S CHILDREN

When Alfred died, he was king of half of England, but Vikings still controlled East Anglia and the lands north of Leicester. It was up to Alfred's children, whom he had with his wife Eahlswith, to expand Alfred's kingdom.

Edward the Elder

On Alfred's death, his oldest son, Edward, and Athelwold, the son of Alfred's brother, both believed they should be king. When Edward was elected king by the Witan (council of nobles and bishops), Athelwold persuaded Vikings in Northumbria and East Anglia to help him fight Edward. The two armies met at Devil's Dyke in Cambridgeshire in around 905. Edward won the battle. It left him as ruler over the land previously controlled by the Vikings.

Devil's Dyke today

Athelflaed

Alfred's daughter, Athelflaed, married the lord of Mercia when she was just 16 years old. She was said to be beautiful, intelligent and very determined. Athelflaed was so well respected that when her husband died, the people of Mercia made her their leader. She led her troops into battle many times, taking back the Viking towns of Derby and Leicester.

■━━━ Athelflaed is shown in this stained-glass window.

A coin showing King Athelstan's head, dating from his reign.

Just like Alfred

Athelstan was the son of Edward the Elder and became king when his father died in 924. He was the first ruler to be called 'king of all England', after defeating Viking, Welsh, Northumbrian and Scottish forces during his lifetime. Athelstan inherited Alfred's love of books and Christian faith. He stopped people trading on a Sunday, a law that stood for hundreds of years. Athelstan also tried to be a fair king, like his grandad. He passed a law which prevented young people from being executed.

HISTORY LINKS

ATHELSTAN WAS THE FIRST ENGLISH KING TO WEAR A CROWN AND HOLD A SCEPTRE AT HIS CORONATION RATHER THAN A HELMET AND SWORD. HE STARTED A TRADITION THAT HAS CARRIED ON TO THIS DAY.

Queen Elizabeth II at her coronation in 1953

Things to do

Athelstan won a great victory at the Battle of Brunanburh in 937. Soon after, a poem was written about the battle.

Find the poem at: https://www.nottingham.ac.uk/ncmh/dna/brunanburh.aspx. Ask an adult to help you read it.

HOW DO WE KNOW?

Alfred earned the title 'great' because he saved England from being taken over by the Vikings. He must have been determined and brave. But what other qualities did he have? What did people at the time say about him and can we always trust what they said?

How do we know about Alfred?

A page from *The Anglo-Saxon Chronicles*

There are two books that tell us a lot about Alfred and the times he lived in.

The Anglo-Saxon Chronicles

Alfred wanted his people to be proud of their history. So he ordered a group of monks to begin writing the history of Britain since the time of Jesus. The book they wrote is called *The Anglo-Saxon Chronicles*. The monks used the writings of a famous historian called St Bede (673–735) to help write their version of Britain's history. We can trust most of what the monks wrote about Alfred because they were alive at the same time as him.

Things to do

Bede was one of the most famous Anglo-Saxon writers.

Find out five facts about Bede, including where he lived and died and the name of his book which was used by the monks who wrote *The Anglo-Saxon Chronicles*.

Bede was known as 'the father of English history'.

Alfred's biography

In 885 Alfred asked a monk called Bishop Asser to write his (Alfred's) life story. He was a clever, well educated man and Alfred and he became friends. Asser was alive at the same time as Alfred so his writings are a good, reliable source of historical information. However, he also admired Alfred, so he may have been kind in what he wrote about him.

King Alfred tests his candle clock.

Things to do

We can work out what Alfred was like by looking at the things he did. Here are five facts about Alfred. Choose the adjectives (see below) that best describe what you think Alfred was like.

1. When he was young, Alfred memorised a book to win it as a prize.

2. At the Battle of Ashdown in 871 Alfred 'fought like a wild boar'. He and his men drove the Vikings back and won a great victory.

3. Alfred defeated the Viking leader Guthrum at the Battle of Edington in 878. Instead of having him killed, Alfred persuaded Guthrum to be baptised as a Christian. Afterwards they feasted together and made a peace agreement.

4. When he was an adult Alfred learned to read Latin so that he could translate important books into English. Alfred wrote out these books by hand as there were no printing machines in those days.

5. Alfred is credited with inventing a new type of candle clock (above).

wise organised weak proud clever brave cool determined shy strong foolish kind determined soft cruel generous

Timeline

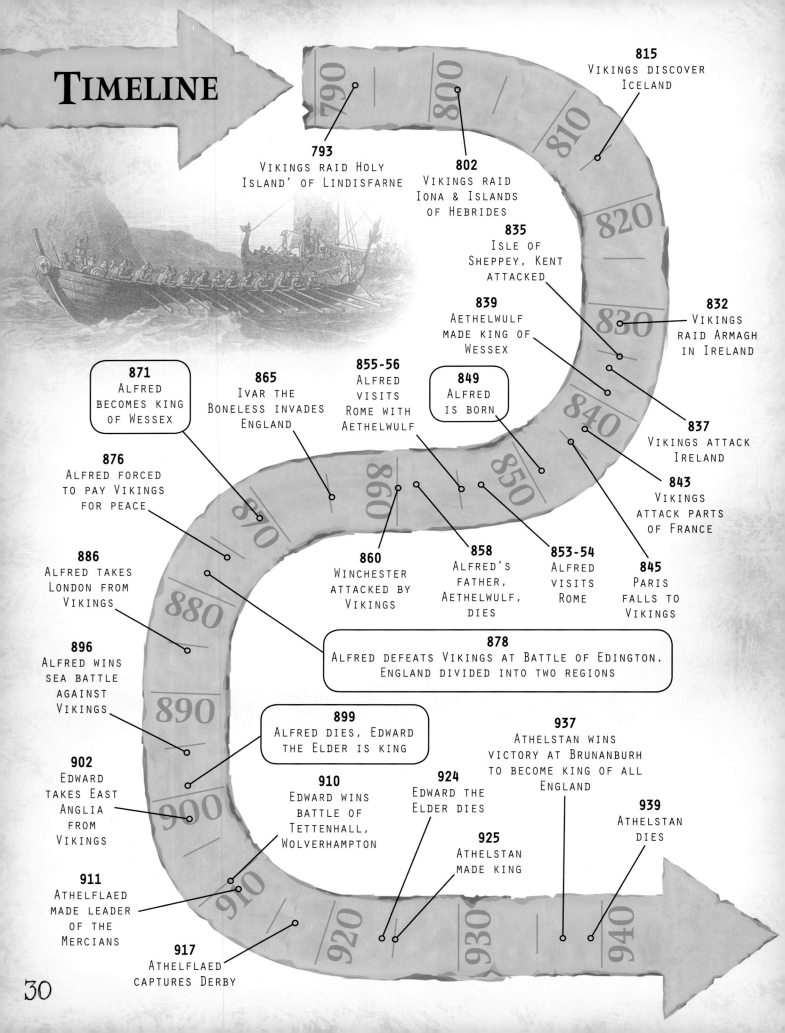

790

793
Vikings raid Holy
Island' of Lindisfarne

800

802
Vikings raid
Iona & Islands
of Hebrides

810

815
Vikings discover
Iceland

820

832
Vikings
raid Armagh
in Ireland

830

835
Isle of
Sheppey, Kent
attacked

839
Aethelwulf
made king of
Wessex

837
Vikings attack
Ireland

840

843
Vikings
attack parts
of France

845
Paris
falls to
Vikings

849
Alfred
is born

850

853-54
Alfred
visits
Rome

855-56
Alfred
visits
Rome with
Aethelwulf

858
Alfred's
father,
Aethelwulf,
dies

860
Winchester
attacked by
Vikings

860

865
Ivar the
Boneless invades
England

871
Alfred
becomes king
of Wessex

870

876
Alfred forced
to pay Vikings
for peace

878
Alfred defeats Vikings at Battle of Edington.
England divided into two regions

880

886
Alfred takes
London from
Vikings

896
Alfred wins
sea battle
against
Vikings

890

899
Alfred dies, Edward
the Elder is king

902
Edward
takes East
Anglia
from
Vikings

900

910
Edward wins
battle of
Tettenhall,
Wolverhampton

911
Athelflaed
made leader
of the
Mercians

910

917
Athelflaed
captures Derby

920

924
Edward the
Elder dies

925
Athelstan
made king

930

937
Athelstan wins
victory at Brunanburh
to become king of all
England

939
Athelstan
dies

940

GLOSSARY

Anglo-Saxons northern European tribes that settled in Britain from the 5th century

Baptise to welcome into the Christian faith

Burh a big town, protected by walls and ditches

Conquer to take over a place by force

Latin the language of ancient Rome and the Roman Empire

Legend an old story that may not be completely true

Monastery a place where monks live

Norse relating to Scandinavia

Pagan a person who does not follow one of the six main faiths

Pilgrimage a journey to a holy place

Prophet a person who is believed to deliver God's words

Raid to attack suddenly

Trade the buying and selling of goods

Vikings Scandinavians who raided the coast of Britain and parts of Europe from the 8th to the 11th centuries. Many later settled in Britain

THE GREAT KING ALFRED QUIZ

THREE CHEERS FOR ALFRED!

1. Who was Alfred's father?

2. In which town did Alfred live and die?

3. Who wrote a book about Alfred's life?

4. How old was Alfred when he first visited Rome?

5. In which year did the Vikings raid Lindisfarne?

6. When Alfred became king of Wessex, what were the names of the other four kingdoms of England?

7. Which Viking leader did Alfred defeat at the Battle of Edington?

8. In what year did Alfred drive out the Vikings from London?

9. Complete this sentence by finding the missing word:

   Alfred translated books from _____ to English.

10. Who decided that Christmas Day should be celebrated on 25 December?

11. Where did Alfred's people, the Anglo-Saxons, come from?

12. What 'title' was given to Alfred's grandson?

Answers on page 32

INDEX

QUIZ ANSWERS

Things to do, page 25

1. I live in this house with my brother. **2.** She is my wife and I love her with all my heart. **3.** I often go home to see my mother.

The Great King Alfred Quiz, page 31

1. Aethelwulf **2.** Winchester **3.** Bishop Asser **4.** Four years old **5.** 793
6. East Anglia, Kent, Mercia and Northumbria **7.** Guthrum **8.** 886
9. Latin **10.** Emperor Constantine **11.** Northern Europe **12.** King of all England